First World War
and Army of Occupation
War Diary
France, Belgium and Germany

57 DIVISION
Headquarters, Branches and Services
Royal Army Veterinary Corps
Assistant Director Veterinary Service
6 February 1917 - 28 February 1919

WO95/2969/6

The Naval & Military Press Ltd
www.nmarchive.com
Published in association with The National Archives

Published by

The Naval & Military Press Ltd

Unit 10 Ridgewood Industrial Park,

Uckfield, East Sussex,

TN22 5QE England

Tel: +44 (0) 1825 749494

www.naval-military-press.com

www.nmarchive.com

This diary has been reprinted in facsimile from the original. Any imperfections are inevitably reproduced and the quality may fall short of modern type and cartographic standards.

© **Crown Copyright**
Images reproduced by permission of The National Archives, London, England, 2015.

Contents

Document type	Place/Title	Date From	Date To
Heading	WO95/2969/6		
Heading	57th Division Asst Dir. Vety Services Feb 1917-Feb 1919		
Miscellaneous	ADVS 57th Division	08/03/1917	08/03/1917
Heading	War Diary Of A.D.V.S. 57th Division From 6th February 1917 To 28th February 1917 (Volume I)		
War Diary	France	06/02/1917	28/02/1917
Heading	War Diary Of A.D.V.S. 57th Division From 1st March 1917 To 31st March 1917 Volume 2		
War Diary	Sailly Sur La Lys	01/03/1917	31/03/1917
Heading	War Diary Of A.D.V.S. 57th Division From 1st April 1917 To 30th April 1917 Volume 3		
War Diary	Sailly Sur La Lys	01/04/1917	30/04/1917
Miscellaneous	Headquarters 57th Division	30/05/1917	30/05/1917
Heading	War Diary Of A.D.V.S, 57th Division From 1st May 1917 To 31st May 1917 Volume 4		
War Diary	Sailly Sur La Lys	01/05/1917	02/05/1917
War Diary	Croix Du Bac	02/05/1917	31/05/1917
Miscellaneous	Headquarters 57th Division	01/07/1916	01/07/1916
Heading	War Diary Of D.A.D.V.S. 57th Division From 1st June 1917 To 30th June 1917 Volume 5		
War Diary	Croix Du. Bac	01/06/1917	30/06/1917
Miscellaneous	A/Q 57th Division	31/07/1917	31/07/1917
Heading	War Diary Of D.A.D.V.S 57th Division From 1st July To 31st July 1917 Volume 6		
War Diary	Croix Du Bac France	01/07/1917	31/07/1917
Miscellaneous	A/Q 57th Division B.E.F.	31/08/1917	31/08/1917
Heading	War Diary Of D.A.D.V.S. 57th Division From 1st Aug 1917 To 31st Aug 1917 Volume VII		
War Diary	Croix Du Bac	01/08/1917	31/08/1917
Miscellaneous	'Q' 57th Division	30/09/1917	30/09/1917
Heading	War Diary Of D.A.D.V.S. 57 Division From 1st Sept To 30th Sept 1917 Volume 8		
War Diary	Norrent-Fontes	01/09/1917	30/09/1917
Heading	War Diary Of D.A.D.V.S. 57th Division From 1/10/17 to 31/10/17 Volume 9		
War Diary	Norrent-Fontes	01/10/1917	31/10/1917
War Diary	Proven	01/10/1917	31/10/1917
War Diary	Elverdinghe	01/10/1917	31/10/1917
Miscellaneous	A/Q 57 Division H.Q	30/11/1917	30/11/1917
Heading	War Diary Of D.A.D.V.S 57th Division From 1st Nov 1917 To 30th Nov 1917 Volume 10		
War Diary	Elverdinghe	01/11/1917	01/11/1917
War Diary	Recques	01/11/1917	30/11/1917
Miscellaneous	A/Q 57 Division H.Q	31/12/1917	31/12/1917
Heading	War Diary Of D.A.D.V.S. 57 Division From 1st Dec 1917 To 31st Dec 1917 Volume 11		
War Diary	Recques	01/12/1917	31/12/1917
War Diary	Proven Rousbrugge	01/12/1917	31/12/1917
War Diary	Elverdinghe	01/12/1917	31/12/1917

Miscellaneous	A/Q 57 Division H.Q	01/02/1918	01/02/1918
Heading	War Diary Of D.A.D.V.S, 57th Division From 1st Jan 1918 To 31st Jan 1918 Volume 12		
War Diary	Elverdinghe	01/01/1918	03/01/1918
War Diary	Steenwerck	03/01/1918	31/01/1918
Miscellaneous	Headquarters 57 Division 'A'/Q'	03/03/1918	03/03/1918
Heading	War Diary Of D.A.D.V.S 57th Division From 1st Feb 1918 To 28th Feb 1918 Volume XIII		
War Diary	Steenwerck	01/02/1918	16/02/1918
War Diary	Merville	16/02/1918	28/02/1918
Heading	War Diary Of D.A.D.V.S 57th Division From 1st March 1918 To 31st March 1918 Volume 14		
War Diary	Merville	01/03/1918	21/03/1918
War Diary	Croix Du Bac	21/03/1918	31/03/1918
Miscellaneous	Headquarters 57 Division 'A'/'Q'	30/04/1918	30/04/1918
Heading	War Diary Of D.A.D.V.S 57th Division 1st To 30th April 1918 Volume 15		
War Diary	Croix Du Bac	01/04/1918	02/04/1918
War Diary	Lucheux	02/04/1918	05/04/1918
War Diary	Couterelle	05/04/1918	09/04/1918
War Diary	Beauquesne	09/04/1918	12/04/1918
War Diary	Lucheux	12/04/1918	13/04/1918
War Diary	Pas	13/04/1918	30/04/1918
Heading	War Diary Of D.A.D.V.S 57th Division From 1st May 1918 To 31st May 1918 Volume 16		
War Diary	Pas	01/05/1918	06/05/1918
War Diary	Couin	06/05/1918	31/05/1918
Miscellaneous	Headquarters 57 Division A/Q	30/06/1918	30/06/1918
Heading	War Diary Of D.A.D.V.S. 57th Division From 1st June 1918 To 30th June 1918 Volume XVII		
War Diary	Couin	01/06/1918	30/06/1918
Heading	War Diary Of D.A.D.V.S 57th Division From 1st July To 31st July 1918 Volume 18		
War Diary	Couin	01/07/1918	02/07/1918
War Diary	Authie	02/07/1918	29/07/1918
War Diary	Bouquemaison	29/07/1918	30/07/1918
War Diary	Hermaville	30/07/1918	31/07/1918
Miscellaneous	Headquarters 57 Division 'A'/'Q'	03/09/1918	03/09/1918
Heading	War Diary Of D.A.D.V.S. 57 Division From 1st Aug 1918 To 31st Aug 1918 Volume 19		
War Diary	Hermaville	01/08/1918	02/08/1918
War Diary	Etrun	02/08/1918	19/08/1918
War Diary	Chelers	19/08/1918	23/08/1918
War Diary	Rebreuve	23/08/1918	24/08/1918
War Diary	Bavincourt	24/08/1918	27/08/1918
War Diary	Mercatel	27/08/1918	31/08/1918
War Diary	Heninel	31/08/1918	31/08/1918
Miscellaneous	H.Q 57 Division "A"	04/10/1918	04/10/1918
Heading	War Diary Of D.A.D.V.S. 57th Division 1st Sept 1918 To 30th Sept 1918 Volume 20		
War Diary	Heninel	01/09/1918	08/09/1918
War Diary	Queant	08/09/1918	17/09/1918
War Diary	Bavincourt	17/09/1918	26/09/1918
War Diary	Queant	26/09/1918	28/09/1918
War Diary	Pronville	28/09/1918	30/09/1918
War Diary	Moeuvres And Fontaine	30/09/1918	30/09/1918

Miscellaneous	H.Q 57 Division	31/10/1918	31/10/1918
Heading	War Diary Of D.A.D.V.S. 57th Division 1st October 1918 To 31st October 1918 Volume 21		
War Diary	Cambrai Between Moeuvres And Fontaine E 28.b.2.7 Sheet 57c	01/10/1918	12/10/1918
War Diary	Barlin	12/10/1918	14/10/1918
War Diary	Epinette	14/10/1918	17/10/1918
War Diary	Fromelles	17/10/1918	18/10/1918
War Diary	Englos	18/10/1918	19/10/1918
War Diary	Petit Ronchin	19/10/1918	21/10/1918
War Diary	Willems	21/10/1918	31/10/1918
Miscellaneous	H.Q 57 Div. 'A'/'Q'	03/12/1918	03/12/1918
Heading	War Diary Of D.A.D.V.S 57th Division 1st Nov 1918 To 30th Nov 1918 Volume 22		
War Diary	Mons-En-Baroeul	01/11/1918	30/11/1918
Miscellaneous	Headquarters 57th Division	04/01/1919	04/01/1919
Heading	War Diary Of D.A.D.V.S 57th Division From 1st Dec. 1918 To 31st Dec.1918 Volume 23		
War Diary	Mons-En-Baroeul	30/11/1918	02/12/1918
War Diary	Duisans	02/12/1918	31/12/1918
Heading	War Diary Of The D.A.D.V.S 57th Division For The Month Of January 1919 Volume XXIV		
War Diary	Duisans	01/01/1919	31/01/1919
Heading	War Diary For Month Ending 28th February 1919 Vol. 25		
War Diary	Duisans	01/02/1919	28/02/1919

W0995/2969/6
Assistant Director Veterinary Services

57TH DIVISION

ASST DIR. VETY SERVICES

FEB 1917 - FEB 1919

From A.D.V.S, 57th Division
To:- D.A.G. 3rd Echelon

Herewith attached War Diary of A.D.V.S. 57th Division, covering the period of 6th February 1917 to 28th Feb: 1917.

[signature]
MAJOR.
A.D.V.S. 57th (WEST LANCS) DIVISION.

57th D.H.Q.
8/3/17.

Army Form C. 2118.

ADVS 57 ² Vol 1

WAR DIARY
or
INTELLIGENCE SUMMARY.
(Erase heading not required.)

Instructions regarding War Diaries and Intelligence Summaries are contained in F. S. Regs., Part II. and the Staff Manual respectively. Title pages will be prepared in manuscript.

Place	Date	Hour	Summary of Events and Information	Remarks and references to Appendices
			Confidential	
			War Diary of	
			A.D.V.S., 54th Division	
			From 6th February 1917. To:- 28th February 1917.	
			(Volume 1.)	

T2134. Wt. W708 -776. 500000. 4/15. Sir J. C. & S.

Army Form C. 2118.

Instructions regarding War Diaries and Intelligence Summaries are contained in F. S. Regs., Part II. and the Staff Manual respectively. Title pages will be prepared in manuscript.

WAR DIARY
or
INTELLIGENCE SUMMARY.
(Erase heading not required.)

Folio 1

Place	Date	Hour	Summary of Events and Information	Remarks and references to Appendices
France	6/2/17		The Division commenced to move from Blackdown on the 6" inst. the last unit arriving in the area of concentration about MERRIS on the 22nd inst.	
	28/2/17		During the move 46 animals died & were disposed 36 from pneumonia. The principal causes of the large number of deaths from pneumonia being the inclement weather during the base periods of the move, the temperature was below freezing point & also the ventilation of trucks in which the animals were subjected. Finally very cold in cattle trucks to Southampton. Several very hot on board ship where some remained for two days. Thirty very cold again in trucks from HARVE & BEUVILLEUL. The journey (which from 30 to 40 hours. All animals being unaccustomed to the French trucks picked & rusted for the first few hours & after wards got very food. Upon arrival at BEUVILLEUL the animals marched to their camps & were picnicked out. A few animals did't notice that the majority the 37 Dir	

Army Form C. 2118.

Folio 2

WAR DIARY
or
INTELLIGENCE SUMMARY.

(Erase heading not required.)

Instructions regarding War Diaries and Intelligence Summaries are contained in F. S. Regs., Part II. and the Staff Manual respectively. Title pages will be prepared in manuscript.

Place	Date	Hour	Summary of Events and Information	Remarks and references to Appendices
			Within a few days of arrival the percentage of unfit amongst these animals which has only recently been obtained from Remounts the animals severely have lost considerably over leaving ENGLAND. The Chargers being first; the journey & secondly the forced ration being much smaller than that which they were obtaining before.	

R.P.Stewart Lt/Major
O. C. S.s. 57 B.s.

Army Form C. 2118.

WAR DIARY
or
INTELLIGENCE SUMMARY.
(Erase heading not required.)

Instructions regarding War Diaries and Intelligence Summaries are contained in F. S. Regs., Part II. and the Staff Manual respectively. Title pages will be prepared in manuscript.

Place	Date	Hour	Summary of Events and Information	Remarks and references to Appendices

Vol 2

CONFIDENTIAL.

WAR DIARY

OF.

A.D.V.S., 57th DIVISION.

FROM 1st MARCH 1917 TO 31st MARCH, 1917.

(VOLUME. 2.)

T2134. Wt. W708-776. 500000. 4/15. Sir J. C. & 9.

WAR DIARY
or
INTELLIGENCE SUMMARY.

Army Form C. 2118.

Place	Date	Hour	Summary of Events and Information	Remarks and references to Appendices
Sailly our la Lys	1/3/17 to 31/3/17		At the commencement of the month the 287th Bde. R.F.A. was broken up. The Howitzer Batteries of the remaining Brigades being made up to six guns. The remainder of the 287 Bde. was posted to other formations. This alteration in establishments caused one veterinary officer in the Division to become surplus & Captain A. Walker A.V.C. consequently left. The health of the animals generally is good, but many animals in the Divisional R.A. are losing condition. The primary causes being :- (a) Bad horsemastership. The officers have to be up at the gun positions & it is seldom one can be found at the wagon lines. (b) The reduction of the forage ration. The R.D. horses were receiving 12 lbs of corn at home, whilst now they only receive about 8¾ lbs. (c) The standings being more often than those they have been in during the winter. (d) The absence of chaff. The batteries which are commanded by officers who take an interest in their animals have been able either to hire chaff cutters or to make arrangements with farmers to have some of the hay chopped.	

A good many animals were affected with cold & catarrh, contracted on the voyage over. Many of these have not been able to pick up again & have become debilitated & have had to be evacuated to Hospital.

Mange. There have been only two cases in the Division during the month both animals were also suffering from debility & were evacuated.

Arrangements have been made for the sale of incurably injured animals to butchers for flesh & skins of those which die to be taken off & sent back to the R.f.q. During the month 12 cathenes have been sold the sum of 1920 francs being credited to the public. Skins of these i.e. Kent, there has been some difficulty in finding purchasers, but in future it is hoped better prices will be obtained.

13 Skins have been sent to the Veterinary Hospital I. of C. As it is not always possible to send a man from the Mobile Veterinary Section to skin the animals, the skins have in some instances been cut, but the majority have been taken off quite well by men in the units.

[signature]
A.D.V.S. 57th WEST LANCS. DIVISION

Army Form C. 2118.

WAR DIARY
or
INTELLIGENCE SUMMARY.
(Erase heading not required.)

Vol 3

Confidential

War Diary

of

A.D.V.S., 57th Division.

from 1st April 1917 to 30th April 1917.

Volume 3.

WAR DIARY
or
INTELLIGENCE SUMMARY.

Army Form C. 2118.

Folio 1

Place	Date	Hour	Summary of Events and Information	Remarks and references to Appendices
SAILLY SUR LA LYS	1/4/17		At the commencement of this month the condition of the animals of the 57 Divisional R.A. was getting very bad. Due principally to bad horsemastership & careless supervision of the battery officers. The following steps were taken to deal with the matter with very good results. An officer was placed in charge of each battery wagon lines & orders were issued that he was not to be relieved until the animals' harness. The poor conditioned animals were parted with & crosse by the veterinary officers & kept together for special feeding & attention. These animals where sent out for walking exercise daily & allowed to do no draught work. The condition of the animals in each battery was published in Divisional Orders. The latter appears to do more good than anything else, as the Battery Commanders disliked more than anything to see it in print that their animals were bad, & then did their best to improve matters	
	30/4/17		On the 12th went an allowance of 10 centimes a day per horse was sanctioned to be spent on Extra foods. With this money carrots Cab.	

T2134. Wt. W708—776. 500000. 4/15. Sir J. C. & S.

WAR DIARY or INTELLIGENCE SUMMARY.

Army Form C. 2118.

Folio 2

Cake & grass were purchased which did a lot of good to the debilated animals.

On 22nd inst all animals were put on full rations which together with the warmer weather has caused much improvement.

During the month 73 animals were evacuated from the R.A. for debility which from all other units of this Division only four were sent away for this cause.

The wastage has been very heavy considering that the animals have practically being doing no work.

Contagious diseases. There have been two cases of mange but no other outbreak of any sort.

R.S. Ryan Capt
ADVS. 37 Division

30.4.17

Confidential.

A.D.V.S.
V349
Date 31/5/17
57th WEST LANCASHIRE DIVISION

Headquarters,
57 Division.

Herewith attached Confidential War Diary for the month of May, for favour of transmission to the D.A.G. G.H.Q. 3rd Echelon, please.

[signature]

MAJOR.
A.D.V.S. 57th (WEST LANCS.) DIVISION.

D.HQ.
30/5/17

Copy to O. i/c A.V.C. Base Records.

Army Form C. 2118.

WAR DIARY
or
INTELLIGENCE SUMMARY.
(Erase heading not required.)

Vol 4

CONFIDENTIAL

WAR DIARY

OF

A.D.V.S., 57th DIVISION

from 1st MAY 1917 to 31st MAY 1917.

(VOLUME 4)

Army Form C. 2118.

WAR DIARY
or
INTELLIGENCE SUMMARY.
(Erase heading not required.)

Folio I.

Instructions regarding War Diaries and Intelligence Summaries are contained in F.S. Regs., Part II. and the Staff Manual respectively. Title pages will be prepared in manuscript.

Place	Date	Hour	Summary of Events and Information	Remarks and references to Appendices
SAILLY SUR LA LYS	1/5/17 to 2/5/17		The Headquarters of the 57th Division moved to CROIX DU BAC on 2nd May 1917; the Wagon Lines of the Divisional Units remaining in the same position.	
CROIX DU BAC	2/5/17 to 31/5/17		On the 20th instant, the Division was transferred from the II Anzac Corps, Second Army to the XI Corps, First Army; the position still remaining the same. The administration of the Sick Horse Barge Service from ESTAIRES to FRANCE to be continued by the A.D.V.S., 57th Division; places to be allotted on barge to D.D.V.S., Second Army should be require any. The number of animals evacuated has fallen considerably, the average number being about ten (10) per week from this Division. During the month eight (8) animals have received gunshot wounds four (4) of which died. The condition of the majority of the animals is very good, and their health excellent. There is no contagious disease, and the sick cases are only suffering from minor injuries such as kicks. The	

Army Form C. 2118.

WAR DIARY
or
INTELLIGENCE SUMMARY.

(Erase heading not required.)

Folio II

Instructions regarding War Diaries and Intelligence Summaries are contained in F. S. Regs., Part II. and the Staff Manual respectively. Title pages will be prepared in manuscript.

Place	Date	Hour	Summary of Events and Information	Remarks and references to Appendices
			number of cases of "Packed u/p nails" is decreasing considerably owing no doubt to more care being taken at the dumps. All units either have chaff cutting machines, or have made arrangements to have a certain amount of the hay and straw chaffed.	

J Aryle Smith
MAJOR.
A.D.V.S, 57th (WEST LANCS) DIVISION.

CONFIDENTIAL

Headquarters
57th Division.

In accordance with Field Service Regulations, Part II para 140, herewith attached Confidential War Diary covering June 1917, for transmission to the A.G's office at the Base.

A duplicate of the Diary has been forwarded for safe custody to the

Officer i/c A.V.C Records.
WOOLWICH.

57th DHQ,
1-7-16.

MAJOR,
D.A.D.V.S. 57TH (WEST LANCS.) DIVISION.

Army Form C. 2118.

Vol 5

WAR DIARY
or
INTELLIGENCE SUMMARY.
(Erase heading not required.)

Instructions regarding War Diaries and Intelligence Summaries are contained in F. S. Regs., Part II. and the Staff Manual respectively. Title pages will be prepared in manuscript.

Place	Date	Hour	Summary of Events and Information	Remarks and references to Appendices

CONFIDENTIAL

WAR DIARY

OF

D.A.D.V.S. 57th DIVISION

From 1st JUNE 1917 to 30th JUNE 1917

(VOLUME 5).

Army Form C. 2118.

Folio I

WAR DIARY
or
INTELLIGENCE SUMMARY.
(Erase heading not required.)

Instructions regarding War Diaries and Intelligence Summaries are contained in F.S. Regs., Part II. and the Staff Manual respectively. Title pages will be prepared in manuscript.

Place	Date	Hour	Summary of Events and Information	Remarks and references to Appendices
CROIX-DU-BAC	1/6/17 to 30/6/17		The health and condition of the animals remain good; there being no cases of infectious or contagious disease. The Divisional Horse Show was held on the 18th instant. The condition of all the animals shown was excellent. Prior to the Horse Show, preliminary inspections were held of all animals in each Unit in order to eliminate any unit from the Show whose horses generally were not in good condition, and thus present an unit spending all its time on those animals which it intended showing, to the detriment of the others. The following is a copy of Divisional Routine Order No 891 dated 19-6-17 :— " The G.O.C. is glad to notice that the General Condition of the horses of the Division is satisfactory. The 2/2 Wessex Field Ambulance obtained 100% of marks at the inspection preliminary	

Army Form C. 2118.

WAR DIARY
or
INTELLIGENCE SUMMARY.
(Erase heading not required.)

Folio II

Place	Date	Hour	Summary of Events and Information	Remarks and references to Appendices
			"In the Horse Shoe."	
			On the 1st instant, all animals were moved from shelters and stables to open lines, there having been practically no rain; the lines have been kept in good condition.	
			The principal cause of casualties during the month has been "Shell Fire"; 21 animals having died, and 12 were evacuated, from and for this cause.	
			The 421 St Field Coy R.E. lines were shelled on the night of the 8/9 instant, the shell fire causing 15 animals to die, and 9 others had to be evacuated for wounds.	

(Volume 5)

B. Smyth Pigott
MAJOR.
D.A.D.V.S. 57th (WEST LANCS) DIVISION

War Diary for July 1917

D.A.D.V.S.
57th DIVISION.

A/Q 57th Division
O. i/c A.V.C. Records.

Herewith attached Confidential War Diary for July 1917.

[signature]
MAJOR,
D.A.D.V.S. 57th DIVISION

57 D.H.Q.
31·7·17

Army Form C. 2118.

WAR DIARY
or
INTELLIGENCE SUMMARY.
(Erase heading not required.)

Vol 6

CONFIDENTIAL

WAR DIARY

OF

D.A.D.V.S. 57th DIVISION

from 1st July to 31st July 1917

(VOLUME 6.)

Army Form C. 2118.

WAR DIARY
or
INTELLIGENCE SUMMARY.
(Erase heading not required.)

Folio I

Instructions regarding War Diaries and Intelligence Summaries are contained in F. S. Regs., Part II. and the Staff Manual respectively. Title pages will be prepared in manuscript.

Place	Date	Hour	Summary of Events and Information	Remarks and references to Appendices
CROIX-DU-BAC FRANCE	1/1/17 to 3/1/17		On the night of 2nd/3rd instant the Wagon Lines of No 2 Section 57th D.A.C. were bombed by enemy aircraft resulting in seventy-one (71) Casualties to the Animals; of which forty (40) were either killed outright, or had to be shot, and 21 evacuated to L. of C. Veterinary Hospital. The aeroplanes returned again the same night after all animals which could walk had been removed, and dropped more bombs on the horse lines. On the night of the 6th instant, enemy aeroplanes again bombed the same Camp, but the animals having been put into stables only one horse was slightly injured. On the 7th instant, this Camp was evacuated. All animals of the Division are now in very good condition with the exception of D/285 Bde R.F.A. This Battery has never been good; even in England the condition of the animals was always below that of other Units	

WAR DIARY
or
INTELLIGENCE SUMMARY.

Army Form C. 2118.

Folio II

(Erase heading not required.)

Place	Date	Hour	Summary of Events and Information	Remarks and references to Appendices
			During the month there has been three (3) cases of mange. The animals affected were received from BOULOGNE, and showed no visible lesions for over three (3) weeks after arrival. They were, no doubt, "rechauffé" cases. All three cases were evacuated.	
			On the 15th instant Capt. H.A. THORNE A.V.C.(T.F.) was evacuated to the C.C.S. for "Debility" and owing to the reductions in Establishment, this Officer will not be replaced.	
			On the 30th instant four (4) animals were affected by the new German Gas whilst in ARMENTIERES; the symptoms being up to the present only "acute Conjunctivitis" with a muco-purulent discharge.	

MAJOR.
D.A.D.V.S. 57th DIVISION

D.A.D.V.S.,
57th DIVISION.

A/Q 57 Division, B.E.F.
O. i/c A.V.C. Records, Woolwich.

Herewith attached AF C 2118 (Confidential War Diary) for the month of August, 1917, in accordance with F.S. Regulations Part II para 140.

57 D.H.Q.
31. 8. 17

MAJOR,
D.A.D.V.S. 57th DIV.

Army Form C. 2118.

WAR DIARY
or
INTELLIGENCE SUMMARY.
(Erase heading not required.)

CONFIDENTIAL

WAR DIARY

OF

D.A.D.V.S. 54th DIVISION

from 1st Aug. 1917 to 31st Aug. 1917

(Volume VII)

WAR DIARY
or
INTELLIGENCE SUMMARY.
(Erase heading not required.)

Army Form C. 2118.

Folio I

Place	Date	Hour	Summary of Events and Information	Remarks and references to Appendices
CROIX DU BAC	1/8/17 to 31/8/17		On the night of the 29th/30th July and during the following day ARMENTIERES was heavily shelled with "mustard" Gas Shells. Four animals only were gassed at this time. The gas had an irritant effect on the mucous membranes and on that part of the body sparsely covered with hair, such as the muzzle, sheath, and perineum. The animals affected showed acute conjunctivitis with a muco-purulent discharge, the eyes being quite closed and very painful. After a few days the inflammation of the conjunctiva subsides, and the animals then showed acute "Keratitis" and were quite blind. The skin peeled around the nostrils and anus. These animals showed no systematic disturbance, and never went off feed. Two of these animals were kept for a fortnight, and two for three weeks, and as the eyes did not improve, they were evacuated to Hospital. A horse belonging to a Civilian, which was "gassed" at the same time, and longer in the gas, in addition to the symptoms showed by	

Army Form C. 2118.

Folio II

WAR DIARY
or
INTELLIGENCE SUMMARY.
(Erase heading not required.)

the other animals had also "Laryngitis" and "acute inflammation of the mucus membrane lining the nostrils", which caused a certain amount of difficulty in breathing.

Owing to the gas having practically no smell, or that the smell was not recognised, gas masks were not put on any of the animals.

On the night of the 20th instant, four mules and one light draught horse of the 2/4th K.L.R. were killed by shell fire in ERQUINGHEM, and one severely wounded.

On the night of the 22nd instant "A"/285 Battery R.F.A. wagon lines were bombed by enemy aircraft. Two horses were killed and seven injured, one of which had to be destroyed. On the same night the horse lines of the 2/4th L.N.L. Regt were also bombed, four animals being injured.

The health and condition of the animals of the Division remain very good.

During the month there have been five cases of mange, four of

WAR DIARY
or
INTELLIGENCE SUMMARY.
(Erase heading not required.)

Army Form C. 2118.

Folio III

Place	Date	Hour	Summary of Events and Information	Remarks and references to Appendices
			which were Remounts, and the fifth an animal which had been stabled in ARMENTIERES, where, no doubt, it caught the infection.	
			The number of animals on Sick Lines suffering from Kicks is large, due to insufficient care being taken by O's. C. units in isolating known Kickers.	

[signature]
MAJOR.
D.A.D.V.S. 57th DIVISION

D.A.D.V.S.
57TH DIVISION.

"Q" 57th Division.

Officer i/c A.V.C. Records, Woolwich.

———

Herewith attached Confidential War Diary for the month of September 1917, in accordance with F.S. Regns, part II, para 140.

[signature]
MAJOR.
D.A.D.V.S. 57th

14

57th D.H.Q.
30.9.17.

Army Form C. 2118.

WAR DIARY
or
INTELLIGENCE SUMMARY.
(Erase heading not required.)

DADVS 57 D

95 8

CONFIDENTIAL

WAR DIARY

OF

D.A.D.V.S., 57 DIVISION.

FROM 1st SEPT TO 30th SEPT 1917.

(VOLUME 8.)

Army Form C. 2118.

Folio I

WAR DIARY
or
INTELLIGENCE SUMMARY.
(Erase heading not required.)

Instructions regarding War Diaries and Intelligence Summaries are contained in F. S. Regs., Part II. and the Staff Manual respectively. Title pages will be prepared in manuscript.

Place	Date	Hour	Summary of Events and Information	Remarks and references to Appendices
NORRENT-FONTES.	1/9/17 to 30/9/17		The H.Q. of the 57th Division moved from CROIX DU BAC to NORRENT-FONTES on the 14th instant; the Infantry groups following on the 18th, 19th and 20th instant, and the Div. R.A on the 22nd instant. The condition of the animals of the Division continues to be very good, casualties slight, and contagious disease practically nil, there having been only (3) three isolated cases of mange during the month. Each case of mange was seen in its very early stage, and immediately evacuated. All animals are now picketted in the open, there being no covered shelters in this area.	

MAJOR.
D.A.D.V.S. 57th

Army Form C. 2118.

WAR DIARY
or
INTELLIGENCE SUMMARY.
(Erase heading not required.)

WB 9

CONFIDENTIAL

WAR DIARY

of

D.A.D.V.S., 57th DIVISION

from 1·10·17 to 31·10·17.

(Volume 9)

Army Form C. 2118.

WAR DIARY
or
INTELLIGENCE SUMMARY.
(Erase heading not required.)

Folio 1.

Instructions regarding War Diaries and Intelligence Summaries are contained in F. S. Regs., Part II. and the Staff Manual respectively. Title pages will be prepared in manuscript.

Place	Date	Hour	Summary of Events and Information	Remarks and references to Appendices
NORRENT-FONTES	1/10/17 to 31/10/17		On the 6th instant the 57th Div. Artillery accompanied by No 1 Coy of the 57 Div. Train left this area for the XIV Corps, Fifth Army area near ELVERDINGHE. Capt. E.R.H. WOODCOCK A.V.C. and Lieut H.A. DICKINSON A.V.C. went with them, in Veterinary charge. On the 18th instant, the 57 Div. and the three (3) Infantry Brigade groups proceeded to the PROVEN area XIV Corps. On the 25th instant, 57 Div. H.Q. moved to ELVERDINGHE. On this date the 57 Div. Artillery again came under my Veterinary administration. On the 27th instant, I inspected the Artillery Brigades, the animals of which were in good condition when they left NORRENT-FONTES area. I found that the animals had been working very hard, carrying packs of ammunition to the Gun-positions. They had gone down very much in condition, and many were debilitated. The horse lines were in a	
PROVEN				
ELVERDINGHE				

WAR DIARY
or
INTELLIGENCE SUMMARY.
(Erase heading not required.)

Army Form C. 2118.

Folio 2.

Place	Date	Hour	Summary of Events and Information	Remarks and references to Appendices
			Very bad condition; the animals standing nearly up to their knees and hocks in mud; also they were not getting chaff, and were feeding the hay from the ground, owing to the shortage of hay-nets. Chaff machines have now been issued, and some hay nets supplied. Battle casualties have been heavy; a large number of animals reported missing have been lost at or near the gun-positions. The condition of the animals of the other Units in the Division is very good. There has only been one case of Contagious Skin disease during the month. On the 27th instant the 57 Division was transferred to the XIX Corps, 57th remaining in the same area.	

MAJOR,
D.A.D.V.S. 57th DIVISION

A/Q 57 Division H.Q. ✓
O. i/c A.V.C Records, Woolwich.

Herewith attached A.F. C2118 (Confidential War Diary) for period covering 1st Nov. 1917 to 30th Nov. 1917 in accordance with F.S. Regulations para 140.

57 D.H.Q.
30-11-17

MAJOR,
D.A.D.V.S. 57th DIVISION

Vol. 10

CONFIDENTIAL

WAR DIARY

of

D.A.D.V.S., 57th DIVISION

from 1st Nov. 1917 to 30th Nov. 1917.

(Volume 10).

Army Form C. 2118.

Folio I.

WAR DIARY
or
INTELLIGENCE SUMMARY.
(Erase heading not required.)

Instructions regarding War Diaries and Intelligence Summaries are contained in F. S. Regs., Part II. and the Staff Manual respectively. Title pages will be prepared in manuscript.

Place	Date	Hour	Summary of Events and Information	Remarks and references to Appendices
ELVERDINGHE	1/11/7		The wastage from debility amongst animals of the 57th Div. R.A continues to be high, owing to the hard work and bad condition of the standing. On the 5th instant, this Division less the R.A moved into "rest" to the RECQUES area, and is being administered by the XVIII Corps, the R.A being left under the administration of the XIX Corps. Eight (8) men of the 2/1 (W.C) Mobile Veterinary Section were retained by the XIX Corps until the 16th instant. On the 11th instant the R.A were moved to this area and again came under my administration. Many of the animals arrived poor and debilitated — Sixty four (64) were evacuated for this cause to the Base.	
RECQUES	to 30/11/7		There being no horse standings in this area, all the animals of the R.A are picketted on Roads; two thirds of the animals of other units have been put into barns and cart-sheds; the remainder being picketted. The animals are doing very	

Army Form C. 2118.

Folio 2

WAR DIARY
or
INTELLIGENCE SUMMARY.
(Erase heading not required.)

Instructions regarding War Diaries and Intelligence Summaries are contained in F. S. Regs., Part II. and the Staff Manual respectively. Title pages will be prepared in manuscript.

Place	Date	Hour	Summary of Events and Information	Remarks and references to Appendices
			little work, and are picking up in condition very quickly. During the month, there has been no mange or Contagious disease, and very little Cellulitis. The principal Cause, now that Sickness being Debility and Necrosis of the Coronet. how that the animals are again in hard standing, the latter disease has practically ceased.	

MAJOR
D.A.D.V.S. 57th DIVISION

D.A.D.V.S.
57TH DIVISION

No......
Date......

A/Q 57 Division H.Q.

O.i/c A.V.O. Records, Woolwich.

Herewith A.F. C 2118 (Confidential War Diary) for the month of Dec. 1917 in accordance with Field Service Regulations, Part II para 140.

57 D.H.Q.
31-12-17

MAJOR,
D.A.D.V.S. 57th DIVISION

Army Form C. 2118.

WAR DIARY
or
INTELLIGENCE SUMMARY.
(Erase heading not required.)

CONFIDENTIAL

WAR DIARY

of

D.A.D.V.S. 57 DIVISION

From 1st Dec. 1917 to 31st Dec. 1917.

(Volume 11)

Army Form C. 2118.

Folio I

WAR DIARY
or
INTELLIGENCE SUMMARY.
(Erase heading not required.)

Instructions regarding War Diaries and Intelligence Summaries are contained in F. S. Regs., Part II. and the Staff Manual respectively. Title pages will be prepared in manuscript.

Place	Date	Hour	Summary of Events and Information	Remarks and references to Appendices
RECQUES	1/12/17		Upon first arriving in this (RECQUES) Area the horses of the 57 Div. RA picked up a little in condition, but latterly owing to the cold winds and exposed standing, many lost it again, especially those which had been clipped. On the 8th instant the 57 Division moved to PROVEN, and on the 9th instant to ROUSBRUGGE; the 57 Div. RA going on to ELVERDINGHE.	
PROVEN			The 2/1 (WD) Mobile Veterinary Section took over the Rear Section standing at PROVEN, and evacuating for the Rear Area.	
ROUSBRUGGE			On the 18th instant, the remainder of the 57th Division moved to ELVERDINGHE, the 2/1 (WD) M.V.S taking over the XIX Corps Vety C.C.S near International Corner.	
ELVERDINGHE	31/12/17		Since the Division has been away from this (ELVERDINGHE) area, many horse standings have been erected, and all animals of the Division with the exception of the Div. Train are now under cover. These new stables are very warm	

Army Form C. 2118.

WAR DIARY
or
INTELLIGENCE SUMMARY.
(Erase heading not required.)

Folio II

but in many cases, as nothing has been done to the floors, the animals are standing in deep mud.

The condition of the animals generally is good. During the month there have been three (3) isolated cases of mange. Few animals have been evacuated, except for debility.

There has been no Stomatitis, and only a few cases of Ophthalmia.

During the month there have been Six (6) Battle Casualties, (Three (3) Killed and three (3) wounded by Bombs).

M. Ayer
MAJOR,
O.A.D.V.S. 57th DIVISION

"A"/"Q"
57 Division H.Q. ✓

Officer i/c
A.V.C. Records.
Woolwich

Herewith attached A.F. C 2118 (War Diary) for the month of January 1918, in accordance with Field Service Regulations, Part II para 140.

57 D.H.Q.
1.2.18

MAJOR,
D.A.D.V.S. 57th DIVISION

D.A.D.V.S.
57TH DIVISION

Army Form C. 2118.

WAR DIARY
or
INTELLIGENCE SUMMARY.
(Erase heading not required.)

CONFIDENTIAL

WAR DIARY

of

D.A.D.V.S., 57th DIVISION

from 1st Jan. 1918 to 31st Jan. 1918

(Volume 12)

Army Form C. 2118.

WAR DIARY
or
INTELLIGENCE SUMMARY.
(Erase heading not required.)

Instructions regarding War Diaries and Intelligence Summaries are contained in F. S. Regs., Part II. and the Staff Manual respectively. Title pages will be prepared in manuscript.

Place	Date	Hour	Summary of Events and Information	Remarks and references to Appendices
ELVERDINGHE 1.1.18 to 3.1.18			On the 3rd instant the 57th Division moved from ELVERDINGHE to STEENWERCK; the 2/1 (M.G.) M.V.S. moving to IEKIRLEM.	
STEENWERCK 3.1.18 to 31.1.18			During the month the wastage has been very small, only 20 animals being evacuated from this Division, and of which 3 were for mange. With the exception of 4 Batteries of R.A., the condition of the animals is very good, and the health is excellent. All animals are in good standings, and doing very little work. Under these conditions, the cutting down of the corn ration should make no difference to their condition. Battle Casualties:- one (slight wound only).	

[signature]
MAJOR.
D.A.D.V.S. 57th Division

Headquarters
57 Division "A"/"Q"

Officer i/c A.V.C. Records.
Woolwich

Herewith A.F. C 2118 (War Diary) for the month of February 1918, in accordance with F.S. Regns Part II, para 140.

57 D.HQ
3-3-18

MAJOR,
D.A.D.V.S. 57th DIVISION

Army Form C. 2118.

WAR DIARY
or
INTELLIGENCE SUMMARY.
(Erase heading not required.)

Confidential

War Diary

of

D.A.D.V.S. 57th DIVISION

From 1st Feb. 1918 To 28th Feb. 1918

(Volume XIII)

WAR DIARY
or
INTELLIGENCE SUMMARY.
(Erase heading not required.)

Army Form C. 2118.

Folio I

Place	Date	Hour	Summary of Events and Information	Remarks and references to Appendices
STEENWERCK	1-2-18 to 16-2-18		The health and condition of the animals is "good"; the number of sick animals being much below the average for the last 12 months. Of the more important diseases, there have been only two (2) cases of mange, four (4) cases of Cellulitis, and very few cases of Ophthalmia; the average weekly wastage being under 0.2%.	
MERVILLE	16.2.18 to 28-2-18		On the 16th instant the Division moved into rest at MERVILLE.	

MAJOR,
D.A.D.V.S. 57th DIVISION

Army Form C. 2118.

WAR DIARY
or
INTELLIGENCE SUMMARY.
(Erase heading not required.)

CONFIDENTIAL

WAR DIARY

of

D.A.D.V.S. 57th DIVISION

from 1st MARCH 1918 to 31st MARCH 1918

(VOLUME 14).

Army Form C. 2118.

WAR DIARY
or
INTELLIGENCE SUMMARY.
(Erase heading not required.)

Place	Date	Hour	Summary of Events and Information	Remarks and references to Appendices
MERVILLE	1.3.18 to 21.3.18		The Condition and General Health of the animals continue to be good. The Animals having been only on light work, the reduction in the forage ration has not been felt. There have been only two cases of mange, and very little Ophthalmia. On the 21st instant, the Division moved from MERVILLE into line, Headquarters being at CROIX-DU-BAC. Battle Casualties:- One horse killed.	
CROIX-DU-BAC	21.3.18 to 31.3.18			

Signature
MAJOR,
D.A.D.V.S. 57th DIVISION

CONFIDENTIAL 11

D.A.D.V.S.,
57TH DIVISION.

Headquarters
57 Division "A"/"Q" ✓

Officer i/c Records
 A.V.C, Woolwich.

Herewith A.F. C2118 (War Diary) compiled for the month of April 1918 in accordance with F.S. Regs Part II.

57 Div. H.Q.
30. 4. 18.

MAJOR.
D.A.D.V.S. 57th Division

WAR DIARY
or
INTELLIGENCE SUMMARY.

Army Form C. 2118.

Vol 15

CONFIDENTIAL

WAR DIARY

of

D.A.D.V.S. 57th DIVISION

1st to 30th April 1918

(VOLUME 15)

Army Form C. 2118.

WAR DIARY
or
INTELLIGENCE SUMMARY.
(Erase heading not required.)

Folio I

Place	Date	Hour	Summary of Events and Information	Remarks and references to Appendices
CROIX-DU-BAC	1-4-18 to 2-4-18		On the 2nd instant, the 57th Division (less 57th Div. R.A) left CROIX DU BAC for IUCHEUX by train, and was placed in the Third	
IUCHEUX	2-4-18 to 5-4-18		Army Reserve, and being administered by VI Corps. On the 5th instant Divisional Headquarters moved to COUTERELLE;	
COUTERELLE	5-4-18 to 9-4-18		on the 9th instant to BEAUQUESNE; and on the 12th instant to IUCHEUX, and finally settled down at PAS on the 13th instant, being still in the Third Army Reserve, but under the administration of the	
BEAUQUESNE	9-4-18 to 12-4-18		IV Corps. On the 22nd instant, the 2/10 Liverpool Regt. left the Division, and	
IUCHEUX	12-4-18 to 13-4-18		was replaced by the 1st Munster Fusiliers. Upon arrival of the 1st Munster Fusiliers, their animals were found to be in very poor condition, having been continually	
P.A.S	13-4-18 to 30-4-18		on the move for some days. They are now shewing much improvement. The general health and condition of the animals of the Division is good. There have been two cases of mange during the month	

Army Form C. 2118.

Folio II

WAR DIARY
or
INTELLIGENCE SUMMARY.
(Erase heading not required.)

Place	Date	Hour	Summary of Events and Information	Remarks and references to Appendices

month, both animals affected being M.M.P. horses, which had been out on detached duty.

[signature]
MAJOR,
D.A.D.V.S. 57th DIVISION

Vol 16

CONFIDENTIAL

WAR DIARY

OF

D.A.D.V.S. 57th DIVISION

from 1st MAY 1918 to 31st MAY 1918

(VOLUME 16)

Army Form C. 2118.

WAR DIARY
or
INTELLIGENCE SUMMARY.
(Erase heading not required.)

Folio I.

Place	Date	Hour	Summary of Events and Information	Remarks and references to Appendices
PAS	1.5.18 to 6.5.18		The 57th Division (less Artillery) is still in the Third Army Reserve, and administered by IV Corps. On the 6th instant, the Division (less Artillery) went into "Line" in centre of IV Corps Front, the Divisional H.Q. moving to COUIN, and the 2/1 (W. Lancs) Mobile Veterinary Section remaining at PAS.	
COUIN	6.5.18 to 31.5.18		On the 10th instant the 57 Div R.A. re-joined the Division, after having been in the battle of the IYS since 9th April 1918. The horses of the Div. R.A. were in fair condition considering the rough time they had. The mules of the D.A.C. were in very good condition; also the horses of No.1 Coy 57 Div. Train. A new War Establishment for a M.V.S. has been published, reducing the Section by one Staff Sergt. and six privates. The six privates were transferred to No. 4 V.E.S. on 26/5/18. During the month, there have been no cases of contagious diseases. The horses of the R.A. are now improving, and their condition will soon be good. The condition of other animals of the Division is very good.	

[signature]

Headquarters
57 Division A/Q

Officer i/c
AVC Records, Woolwich.

> D.A.D.V.S.
> 57TH DIVISION.
> No................
> Date..............

Herewith AF C2118 (War Diary) for the month of June 1918, in accordance with Field Service Regns Part II para 140.

[signature]

MAJOR,
D.A.D.V.S. 57th DIVISION

30/6/18

Army Form C. 2118.

WAR DIARY
or
INTELLIGENCE SUMMARY.
(Erase heading not required.)

Instructions regarding War Diaries and Intelligence Summaries are contained in F. S. Regs., Part II. and the Staff Manual respectively. Title pages will be prepared in manuscript.

D.A.D.V.S.
57TH DIVISION

Vol 17

CONFIDENTIAL

WAR DIARY

of

D.A.D.V.S. 57th DIVISION

from 1st JUNE 1918 to 30th JUNE 1918.

(VOLUME XVII)

Place	Date	Hour	Summary of Events and Information	Remarks and references to Appendices

WAR DIARY
or
INTELLIGENCE SUMMARY.
(Erase heading not required.)

Army Form C. 2118.

Folio 1

D.A.D.V.S.
57th DIVISION.

Place	Date	Hour	Summary of Events and Information	Remarks and references to Appendices
COUIN	1/6/18 to 30/6/18		The health and condition of the animals of the Division remain "good", the wastage being comparatively small. There have been a few cases of Wounds (gunshot), but no Bomb Casualties. There is no contagious disease. In accordance with G.R.O. No 4252 dated 11th June 1918, the Riding horses of the Mobile Veterinary Section were reduced to eleven (11). On the 21st June 1918, the D.D.V.S. Third Army (Col. W.A. PALLIN) inspected the animals of the Divisional Artillery, and found that their health and condition were very satisfactory. Capt W.D. WILLIAMS A.V.C. left on the 22nd instant for 14 days' leave to England.	

MAJOR.
D.A.D.V.S. 57th DIVISION

Army Form C. 2118.

WAR DIARY
or
INTELLIGENCE SUMMARY.

(Erase heading not required.)

Instructions regarding War Diaries and Intelligence Summaries are contained in F. S. Regs., Part II. and the Staff Manual respectively. Title pages will be prepared in manuscript.

Place	Date	Hour	Summary of Events and Information	Remarks and references to Appendices

CONFIDENTIAL

WAR DIARY

OF

D.A.D.V.S. 54th DIVISION

FROM 1st JULY TO 30th JULY 1916

(VOLUME 18)

WAR DIARY
INTELLIGENCE SUMMARY.

(Erase heading not required.)

Army Form C. 2118.

Folio I.

Place	Date	Hour	Summary of Events and Information	Remarks and references to Appendices
COUIN	1.7.18 to 2.7.18		On 2nd July the Division moved out to rest, Div Headquarters moving to AUTHIE, and the 2/1 (W.Lancs) Mob. Vet. Section to SARTON.	
AUTHIE	2.7.18 to 29.7.18		Leave was granted to Capt E.R.H. WOODCOCK A.V.C. (V.O. i/c 285 Bde RFA) to proceed to U.K. from 9th to 23rd July. On the 27th instant the Division went into G.H.Q. reserve, and moved	
BOURQUEMAISON	29.7.18 to 30.7.18		to BOURQUEMAISON on the 29th instant, the 2/1 (W.Lancs) Mob. Vet. Section also moving there. The D.A.D.V.S (Major P.W. DAYER SMITH A.V.C) was granted Special leave of 14 days to U.K. on 29th instant. On the 30th instant the Division moved to HERMAVILLE, the 2/1 (W.	
HERMAVILLE	30.7.18 to 31.7.18		Lancs) Mob. Vet. Section going to MONTENESCOURT, and on the 31st instant to GOUVES. The condition of all animals except those of the 285th Bde R.F.A. is good, and still improving. There has been no Contagious disease among the Animals, and the wastage has been small.	

W. D. Hill Capt. A.V.C

for MAJOR. (on leave)

D.A.D.V.S, 57th DIVISION

16 CONFIDENTIAL

D.A.D.V.S.
57TH DIVISION

No............
Date...........

Headquarters
57 Division "A"/Q ✓

O. i/c A.V.C. Records
  Woolwich.

Herewith AF C.2118 (War Diary) for the month of August 1918, in accordance with F.S. Rgns Part II para 140.

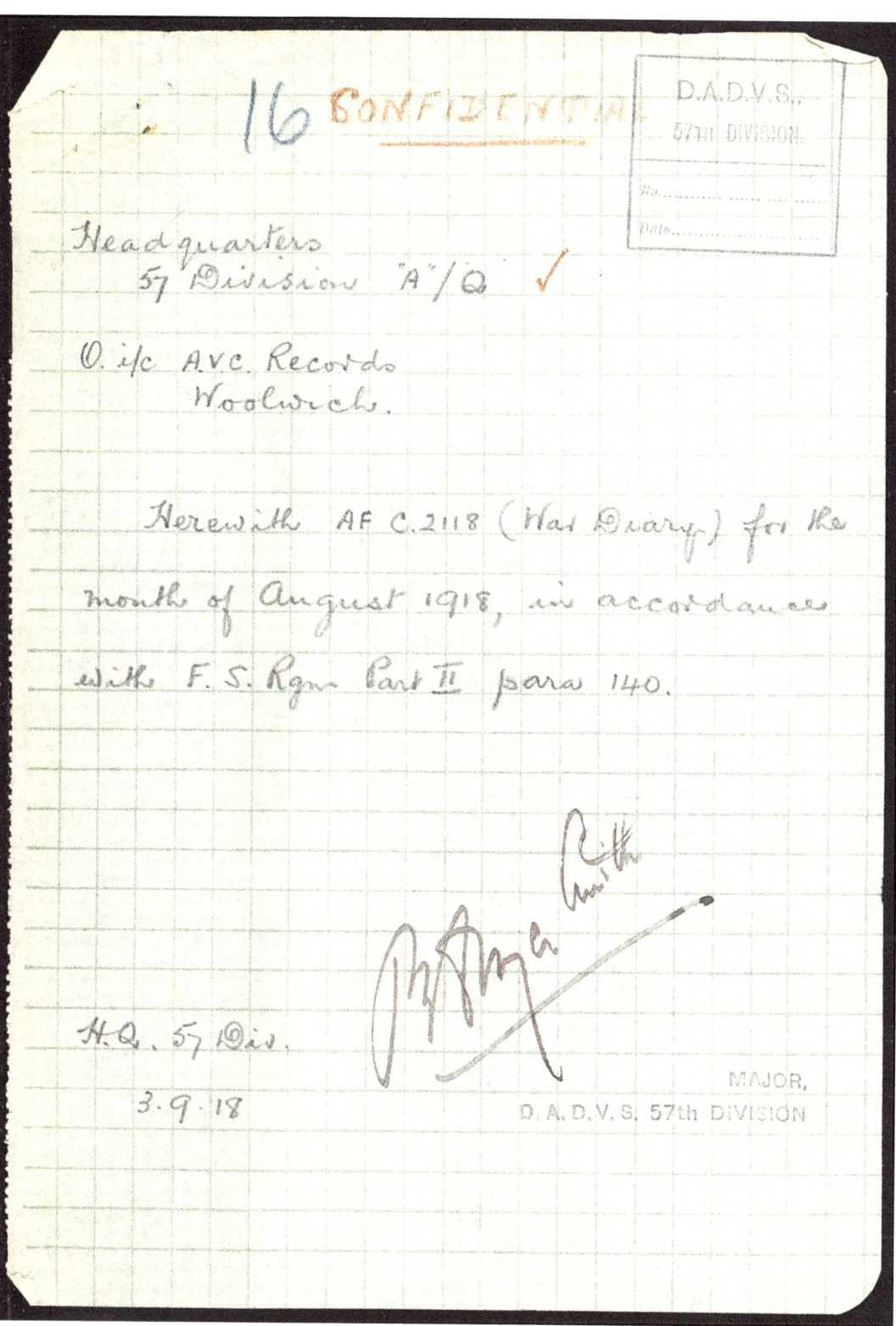

H.Q. 57 Div.
3.9.18

MAJOR,
D.A.D.V.S. 57th DIVISION

Army Form C. 2118.

WAR DIARY
or
INTELLIGENCE SUMMARY.
(Erase heading not required.)

CONFIDENTIAL

WAR

OF

DIARY

D.A.D.V.S. 54 DIVISION

From 1st Aug 1918 To 31st Aug 1918

Volume 19

Army Form C. 2118.

WAR DIARY
or
INTELLIGENCE SUMMARY.

(Erase heading not required.)

Folio I

Instructions regarding War Diaries and Intelligence Summaries are contained in F. S. Regs., Part II. and the Staff Manual respectively. Title pages will be prepared in manuscript.

Place	Date	Hour	Summary of Events and Information	Remarks and references to Appendices
HERMAVILLE	1.8.18 to 2.8.18		On the 2nd instant the Division moved to ETRUN, and remained in Line until the 19th instant. The 2/1 (W.Lancs) Mot Vet. Sec. moving to LARESSET.	
ETRUN	12.8.18 to 19.8.18		On the 12th instant, the D.A.D.V.S. (Major P.W. DAYER SMITH) returned from leave.	
CHELERS	19.8.18 to 23.8.18		On the 19th instant the Division moved out to CHELERS into G.H.Q. Reserve, the 2/1 (W.Lancs) Mot Vet Sec moving to ROCOURT ST LAURENT. On the 23rd the Division moved to REBREUVE in VI Corps area, on the 24th instant	
REBREUVE	23.8.18 to 24.8.18		to BAVINCOURT in XVII Corps, and on the 27th instant to MERCATEL, the Division then going into Line. The 2/1 (W.Lancs) Mot. Vet. Section going to	
BAVINCOURT	24.8.18		BLAIREVILLE. On the 31st instant the Division moved to HENINEL.	
MERCATEL	27.8.18 to 27.8.18 to 31.8.18		There were no Battle Casualties until the 30th instant when the Division Artillery had 60 animals hit by Shellfire and bombs, and of which 26 died or had to be destroyed. Until the Division went into Line	
HENINEL	31.8.18		South of ARRAS the animals were in good Condition, and all improving but after that time during the strenuous work, they began to go down a little. During the month there has been no contagious or infectious diseases. On the 24th instant Capt. A. WHITEHEAD AVC(T.F) (o/c 2/1 W.Lancs mot Vet Sec was granted) special leave to U.K., Capt. W.D. WILLIAMS AVC (T.F) taking charge of the Section during his absence.	

[Signature]
MAJOR.
D.A.D.V.S. 57th DIVISION

CONFIDENTIAL 23   D.A.D.V.S.
                              57TH DIVISION.

H.Q
57 Division "A".

Officer i/c
AVC Record, Woolwich

    Herewith AF C2118 (War Diary) for the month of Sept. 1918, in accordance with F.S. Regns Part II para 1140

                        [signature]
                        Major

H.Q 57 Div
4/10/18   D.A.D.V.S., 57 DIVISION

Army Form C. 2118.

Vol 20

WAR DIARY
or
INTELLIGENCE SUMMARY.
(Erase heading not required.)

CONFIDENTIAL.

WAR DIARY

of

D.A.D.V.S. 57th DIVISION

1st Sept. 1918 to 30th Sept. 1918

(Volume 20)

WAR DIARY or INTELLIGENCE SUMMARY.

Army Form C. 2118.

Folio I

Place	Date	Hour	Summary of Events and Information	Remarks and references to Appendices
HENINEL	1-9-18 to 8-9-18		During the first week of this month the lines were heavily bombed by Enemy Aircraft resulting in 143 Casualties amongst the animals, and of which, 80 either died or had to be destroyed as the result of Shell-fire.	
QUEANT	8-9-18 to 17-9-18		On Sept. 8th the Division moved forward to QUEANT. During this week there were 35 Battle Casualties amongst the animals, and of which 19 were killed.	
BAVINCOURT	17-9-18 to 26-9-18		On Sept 17th the Division moved out to rest in the BAVINCOURT area. On Sept 26th, the Division again went into line, with Headquarters at QUEANT; and on Sept 28th it moved to PRONVILLE, and again on Sept 30th to between MOEUVRES and FONTAINE. On Sept 20th the D.A. left the Div. & joined Canadian Corps in First Army.	
QUEANT	26-9-18 to 28-9-18		During the last week of the month many animals were hit by Shell-fire, but there have been no Casualties from Bombs. There is great difficulty in obtaining sufficient water in the forward area, sufficient water only being erected after the lines have	
PRONVILLE	28-9-18 to 30-9-18			

Army Form C. 2118.

WAR DIARY
or
INTELLIGENCE SUMMARY.

Folio II

(Erase heading not required.)

Place	Date	Hour	Summary of Events and Information	Remarks and references to Appendices
Between MOEUVRES and FONTAINE	30-9-18		have moved on. It has seldom been possible to water the animals more than twice a day, and in consequence they have lost condition. During the month there has been no Contagious disease.	

E. Boyle
Major
D.A.D.V.S., 57 Division

CONFIDENTIAL

D.A.D.V.S.,
57TH DIVISION.

H.Q., 57 Division.
O. i/c A.V.C. Records, Woolwich.

Herewith Confidential War Diary for the month of October 1918, in accordance with Field Service Regns. Part II, para 140.

57 Div. HQ.
31-10-18

[signature]
MAJOR,
D.A.D.V.S. 57th Division.

CONFIDENTIAL

WAR DIARY

of

D.A.D.V.S., 54th DIVISION

1st October 1918 to 31st October 1918.

(Volume 21)

Army Form C. 2118.

WAR DIARY
or
INTELLIGENCE SUMMARY.
(Erase heading not required.)

Folio 1.

Place	Date	Hour	Summary of Events and Information	Remarks and references to Appendices
CAMBRAI between MOEUVRES and FONTAINE E.28.b.2.7 Sheet 57C	1-10-18 to 12-10-18		The Division remained in this area until the 12th instant, the animals doing very hard work. There was little opportunity to graze, and always a certain amount of difficulty to obtain water. A large percentage of the animals were killed during this period from shellfire and bombing. The wastage of animals of the Division (less the Divisional Artillery) for the week ending 10/11th October 1918 amounted to 13.3% mules, 7.2% Horses. On the 12th instant the Division moved to BARLIN (I Corps)	
BARLIN	12-10-18 to 14-10-18		and on the 14th instant moved to EPINETTE near MERVILLE (R.13.d) and joined the XI Corps.	
EPINETTE	14-10-18 to 17-10-18		On the 16th instant, the Divisional Artillery rejoined the Division, having arrived at MERVILLE by train. The animals were in poor condition, and many debilitated. The number of animals were many below authorized strength. On the 17th instant the Division moved to FROMELLES, and on	

T2134. Wt. W708 -776. 500000. 4/15. Sir J. C. & S.

Army Form C. 2118.

WAR DIARY
or
INTELLIGENCE SUMMARY.

(Erase heading not required.)

Folio 2.

Instructions regarding War Diaries and Intelligence Summaries are contained in F. S. Regs., Part II. and the Staff Manual respectively. Title pages will be prepared in manuscript.

Place	Date	Hour	Summary of Events and Information	Remarks and references to Appendices
FROMELLES	17-10-18 to 18-10-18		The 18th instant to ENGLOS, on the 19th instant to PETIT RONCHIN and on the 21st instant to WILLEMS. Since this latter date, the Division has not moved, and half of the Divisional Artillery	
ENGLOS	18-10-18 to 19-10-18		has been resting at ANAPPE, and the animals have improved considerably, many of them standing in quite good German Stables.	
PETIT RONCHIN	19-10-18 to 21-10-18		A considerable amount of forage left in small quantities by the enemy has been collected, and this has helped the forage ration. The condition of the animals generally now is very fair. There has been no contagious disease for many months. Capt. W. A. DICKINSON AVC (TC) was granted leave to the United Kingdom 19th to 21st instant, this leave being extended by the	
WILLEMS	21-10-18 to 31-10-18		D.G., V.S. to the 26th instant on account of sickness.	

[signature]
MAJOR.
D.A.D.V.S. 57th DIVISION

19

H.Q. 57 Div. "A/Q"

Officer i/c
    AVC Records, Woolwich

D.A.D.V.S.,
57TH DIVISION.
No. V 151
Date 5-12-18

Herewith Confidential War Diary (A.F. C2118) for the month of November 1918, in accordance with Field Service Regulations Part II paras 140.

57 Div. H.Q.
3.12.18

[signature]
MAJOR,
D.A.D.V.S. 57th DIVISION

Army Form C. 2118.

WAR DIARY
or
INTELLIGENCE SUMMARY.
(Erase heading not required.)

CONFIDENTIAL

War Diary
of
D.A.D.V.S. 57th Division

1st Nov. 1918 to 30th Nov. 1918.

(Volume 22)

Army Form C. 2118.

WAR DIARY
or
INTELLIGENCE SUMMARY.   Folio I.
(Erase heading not required.)

Instructions regarding War Diaries and Intelligence Summaries are contained in F. S. Regs., Part II. and the Staff Manual respectively. Title pages will be prepared in manuscript.

Place	Date	Hour	Summary of Events and Information	Remarks and references to Appendices
MONS-EN-BARŒUL	1/11/18 to 30/11/18		On 1st Nov. 1918 the Division moved back to rest in the Suburbs on the East side of LILLE; 57 Div. Headquarters being at MONS-EN-BARŒUL, and the 2/1 (W. Lancs) Mobile Veterinary Section at the same place. On the 4th Nov. 1918, the animals of the 57 Div. Artillery were inspected by the D.D.V.S., Fifth Army (Col. Crawford) who stated that they were looking well. On 11th Nov. 1918 an armistice was declared, and the Division has not since moved. All the animals have been stabled under cover, principally in factories which had been used by the enemy. There have been no Battle Casualties or Contagious disease during the month and the animals generally are in Very G__d C__dition [signature] MAJOR, D.A.D.V.S. 57th DIVISION	

CONFIDENTIAL.

Headquarters,
 57th. Division.

Officer i/c R.A.V.C. Records.
 WOOLWICH.

> D.A.D.V.S.,
> 57TH DIVISION.
>
> No............
> Date...........

Herewith A.F.C.2118 (War Diary) for the month of December '18 in accordance with F.S.Regns Part 11 para 140.

H.Q.,57th.Div.
4/1/19.

[signature]

Major.
D.A.D.V.S., 57th.Division.

Army Form C. 2118.

WAR DIARY
or
INTELLIGENCE SUMMARY.

(Erase heading not required.)

C O N F I D E N T I A L.

W A R   D I A R Y

O F

D. A. D. V. S.   57th. D I V I S I O N.

From 1st. Dec. 1918 to 31st. Dec. 1918

(Volume 23)

Army Form C. 2118.

Instructions regarding War Diaries and Intelligence Summaries are contained in F. S. Regs., Part II. and the Staff Manual respectively. Title pages will be prepared in manuscript.

WAR DIARY
or
INTELLIGENCE SUMMARY.
(Erase heading not required.)

Folio 1.

Place	Date	Hour	Summary of Events and Information	Remarks and references to Appendices
MONS-EN-BAROEUL	30-11-18 to 2-12-18		On the 2nd. instant the Division moved from the suburbs of LILLE to the area West of ARRAS ; Divisional Headquarters moving to DUISANS, and the 2/1 (W.Lancs.) Mobile Veterinary Section to its old billet at AGNEZ.	
DUISANS	2-12-18 to 31-12-18		During the month the animals have done very little work, and generally they are in very good condition, there having been practically no sickness On the 6th. instant Capt. W.D.WILLIAMS R.A.V.C.(T.F.) was granted 14 days ordinary leave to the U.K. On the 23rd. instant Capt. E.R.H.WOODCOCK R.A.V.C.(T.F.) was granted 14 days ordinary leave to the U.K.	

[signature]
Major.
D.A.D.V.S., 57th. Division.

Army Form C. 2118.

WAR DIARY
or
INTELLIGENCE SUMMARY.
(Erase heading not required.)

Summary of Events and Information

War Diary

of the

D.A.D.V.S 51st Division

for the month

of

January 1919

Volume XXIV

Army Form C. 2118.

Folio I

WAR DIARY
or
INTELLIGENCE SUMMARY.
(Erase heading not required.)

Place	Date	Hour	Summary of Events and Information	Remarks and references to Appendices
DUISANS	1-1-19 to 31-1-19		During this month there has not been anything of importance to record. Demobilisation of animals is now being proceeded with, & all animals of the Division have been classified into their various groups, & also mallined. The health of the animals in the 51st Division is, generally speaking, good. Major P.W. Dayer Smith O.B.E. (D.A.D.V.S. 51 Division) was granted 14 days ordinary leave to UK as from 27th inst. H.Q. 51 DIV. 1/2/19 W.D. Killi — Capt R.A.V.C for Major D.A.D.V.S 51st Division.	

Army Form C. 2118.

WAR DIARY
or
INTELLIGENCE SUMMARY.
(Erase heading not required.)

4826

DADVS
57 Division

DADVS
57th Division

War Diary
for
month ending
28th February 1919.

Vol. 25

Army Form C. 2118.

WAR DIARY
or
INTELLIGENCE SUMMARY.
(Erase heading not required.)

Place	Date	Hour	Summary of Events and Information	Remarks and references to Appendices
Dunsons	1-2-19 to 28-2-19		Demobilization of the animals is still being proceeded with. All animals in "Y" group have been sent to the Base for repatriation. Only 50 of "Z" group have been sold in this area, but sales have been arranged for, for the remainder. Owing to drivers being demobilized quicker than the animals, the majority of the horses & mules have a dirty & uncared for appearance, there are many more cases of lice.	
H.Q. 57 Div.				

MAJOR,
D.A.D.V.S. 57th DIVISION